# Medical Pioneers

## BY EVELYN BROOKS

## Table of Contents

# What Is a Pioneer?

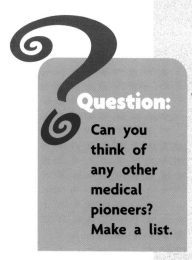

**Question:**

Can you think of any other medical pioneers? Make a list.

A pioneer is someone who does something that no one has done before. Pioneers have courage. Pioneers take risks. Often they fail and try again. They keep going forward even when others think they should stop.

The people you will meet in this book were pioneers in medicine. Florence Nightingale was the first to make nursing a **branch** of the **medical profession**. Jonas Salk was the first to find a way to prevent a crippling disease. Michael DeBakey was the first to find ways to repair a weak heart. Each of these medical pioneers saved thousands of lives.

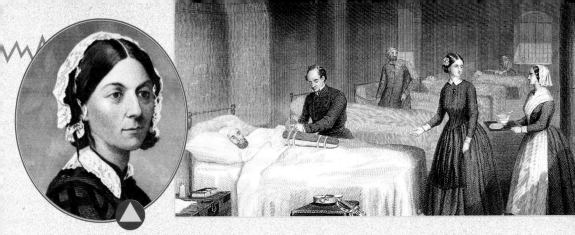

Florence Nightingale: Pioneer in nursing

Jonas Salk, M.D.: Pioneer in vaccine research

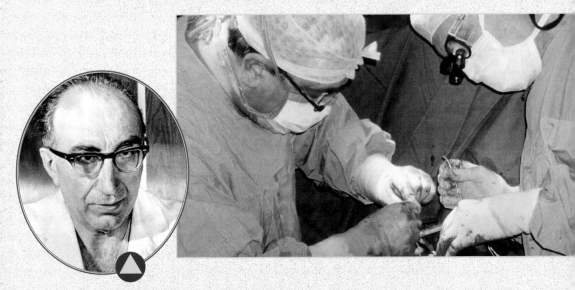

Michael DeBakey, M.D.: Pioneer in heart surgery

# Florence Nightingale *Pioneer in Nursing*

**Florence Nightingale
(1820–1910)**

EUROPE

Italy

Today nurses, along with doctors, take care of the sick. In fact, the word "nurse" means "to take care of." One hundred and fifty years ago, nurses did not care for people in the hospital. Back then they swept floors, emptied bedpans, and did the laundry. In the mid-1800s, one woman changed all that. Her name was Florence Nightingale.

Florence Nightingale was born in Florence, Italy, while her wealthy English parents were traveling in Europe. As a child she traveled to many places with her family and learned how to speak several languages.

When Nightingale was seventeen, she told her family that she was going to help sick people. Her parents did not approve, but Nightingale was determined.

This painting shows an English hospital in 1808.

She traveled to hospitals all over Europe. She saw that doctors were working too hard. She saw that patients died because they did not get enough care. Nightingale felt that women could be doing more to help doctors take care of sick people.

Nightingale knew that in order for nurses to do more, they needed special training in how to take care of sick people. Nightingale went to a hospital in Germany to study nursing. Then she returned to London and became the head of a group of women called Gentlewomen During Illness. These women cared for sick people in their homes.

This painting is *The Hospital Visit* by Manuel Jimenez Prieto. It shows a group of medical students watching a doctor examine a patient.

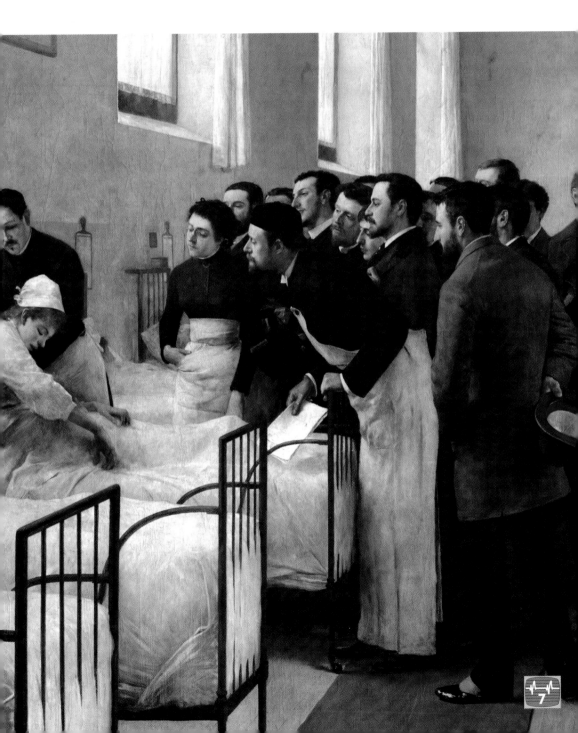

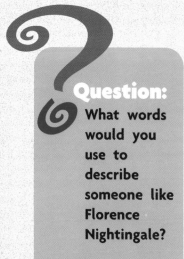

**Question:**
What words would you use to describe someone like Florence Nightingale?

Florence Nightingale tends a wounded soldier during a battle in the Crimean War.

In 1854, England was fighting the Crimean War with Russia. War reporters wrote about the terrible conditions in the hospitals that cared for the wounded. People demanded that something be done about it. A leader of the government asked Florence Nightingale to take some nurses into the war hospitals. So in November 1854, Nightingale finally got to work in a hospital.

She took along thirty-eight nurses whom she had trained herself.

At first the doctors on the battlefields did not want Nightingale and her nurses in their hospitals. They did not believe that women could help. But in fact, the nurses did make a difference. They worked around the clock, tending the sick. Thanks to their hard work, many wounded soldiers survived.

After the war, Nightingale and her nurses were treated like heroes. Finally, in 1860, she started the Nightingale School for Nurses. In time, thanks to Florence Nightingale, nursing became an important part of medicine.

## THE LADY WITH THE LAMP

Each night, walking a total of four miles from bed to bed, Florence Nightingale checked on her wounded soldiers. She was known as "the lady with the lamp" because of the lamp that she carried.

# Jonas Salk *Pioneer in Vaccine Research*

**Jonas Salk
(1914–1995)**

UNITED STATES

New York

In the 1940s and 1950s, a disease called **polio** made thousands of people sick. These people suffered greatly. Some could no longer walk. Others could not even breathe on their own. They had to live the rest of their lives inside a breathing machine called an **iron lung.**

Polio is caused by a germ called a **virus**. People catch polio in the same way they catch a cold, but polio is far more dangerous. There was no way to prevent it until a man named Jonas Salk made an important discovery.

Jonas Salk was born in 1914 in New York City. He was the oldest of three sons. His mother came from Russia.

Neither of his parents ever finished high school, but they made sure that their children were well educated. When Salk was young, he wanted to be a lawyer. While he was in college, however, he changed his mind. He decided to go into medical research.

Here is Jonas Salk (standing, right) with his family.

After Salk finished medical school, he worked in a research lab. He studied influenza (flu) viruses and developed **vaccines** to control them. The vaccines Salk worked on were different from other virus vaccines.

Before that time, virus vaccines were made with living viruses that were weakened so they would cause only a very mild case of the disease. The vaccines Salk worked on were made with viruses that had been killed, so they could never cause the disease.

Dr. Salk looks at a bottle filled with polio viruses.

## A TIME OF FEAR

One of the most famous people to suffer from polio was Franklin D. Roosevelt. Despite being disabled by the disease, he became president of the United States. Roosevelt led the nation from a wheelchair.

Here is President Franklin Delano Roosevelt at his home in New York.

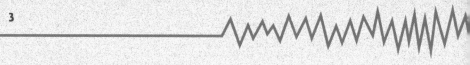

## Question:

Have you ever tried to do something that you weren't sure you would be able to do? How did you feel at that time? How did you feel afterward?

During the polio **epidemics**, doctors needed a vaccine to stop the polio virus from causing disease. It was hard to make a polio vaccine from live virus. Scientists were worried about infecting people with even a weakened virus, just in case it made them sick.

Salk decided to create a safe polio vaccine using killed virus. Other scientists did not believe that he could do it. Even Salk wasn't sure.

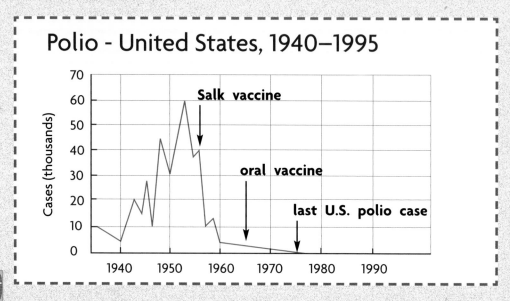

Polio - United States, 1940–1995

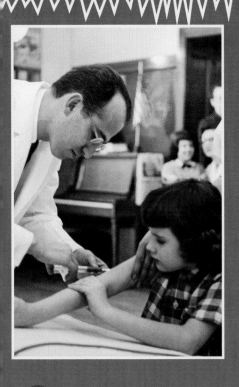

## HOW A VACCINE WORKS

The body has a system that protects it from viruses and other germs that cause disease. It's called the **immune** system. When a person has a disease caused by a germ, the immune system fights it off. The next time the same germ infects that person, the immune system remembers the germ and quickly destroys it. This is called being immune.

A vaccine is given to a person by injection or by mouth in order to prevent a disease. It makes the immune system remember one kind of germ without causing the disease. A person who receives a vaccine becomes immune to the disease and will not become sick if later exposed to it.

Dr. Salk gives a young girl the polio vaccine.

But by 1955 he did it! He made a harmless vaccine that prevented polio. This vaccine saved thousands of lives.

Several years later, another live virus vaccine was made. It was an oral vaccine—it could be swallowed instead of injected. This live vaccine and Salk's killed vaccine brought polio under control. The live polio vaccine was easy to take, but caused some people to get polio. Salk's killed-virus vaccine is the only polio vaccine now used in the United States.

# Michael DeBakey *Pioneer in Heart Surgery*

**Michael E. DeBakey (1908–)**

UNITED STATES

Louisiana

The heart is the body's strongest **organ**. But sometimes parts of the heart become weak, so the heart can no longer do its job. When the heart fails, the body dies.

Now, thanks to the discoveries of Dr. Michael DeBakey, patients with weak hearts can live longer and healthier lives.

Michael DeBakey was born in Lake Charles, Louisiana, in 1908. As a child, DeBakey was an excellent student. He also took top prizes in gardening contests, enjoyed sports, and played in the school band. DeBakey's parents were immigrants and neither of them went to college. But they made sure that all of their children had a good education.

# The Human Heart

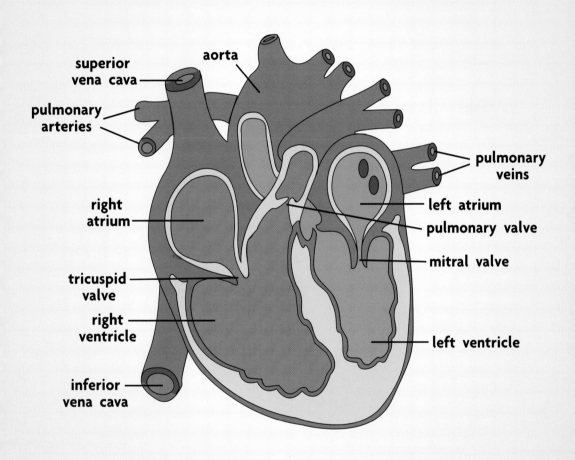

superior
vena cava

aorta

pulmonary
arteries

pulmonary
veins

right
atrium

left atrium

pulmonary valve

tricuspid
valve

mitral valve

right
ventricle

left ventricle

inferior
vena cava

 oxygen-rich blood

 oxygen-poor blood

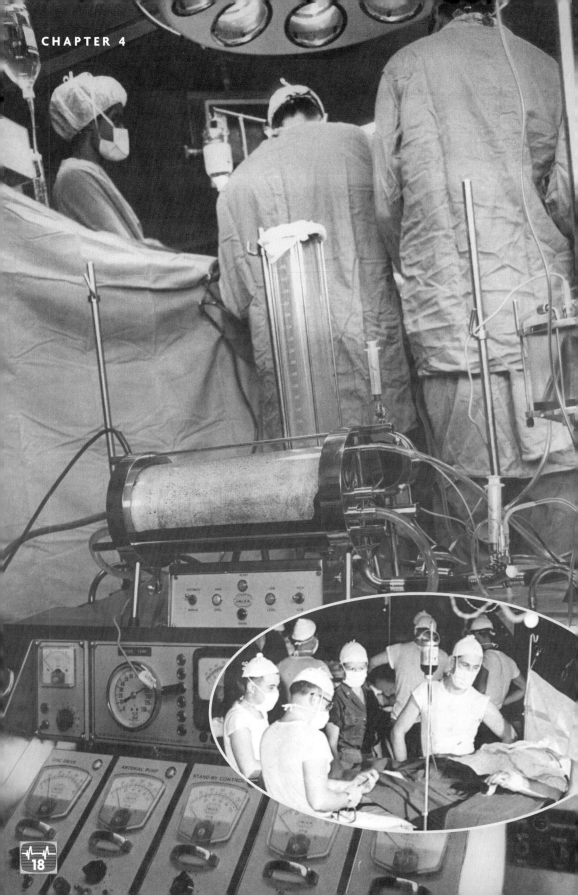

The heart-lung machine keeps the blood flowing through the body while surgeons operate on the heart.

DeBakey entered medical school in 1928. He soon became one of the top students in his class. He was invited to work in the medical laboratory of a famous **surgeon**. There DeBakey developed a machine called a roller-pump. Years later the pump was used to make a heart-lung machine. This machine pumps blood throughout the body while the patient's heart is being repaired.

The roller-pump was just the beginning. In 1942, DeBakey joined the army, working for the medical division. After the war he developed Mobile Army Surgical Hospital (MASH) units. These units saved thousands of soldiers' lives during the Korean and Vietnam wars.

After the war, DeBakey continued to research methods for improving heart **surgery**. In 1950 he developed an **artificial** artery. This device allowed blood to flow around, or bypass, an artery that was blocked with fatty tissue.

During World War II, temporary hospitals were set up close to where soldiers were fighting. These enabled wounded soldiers to get quick medical attention.

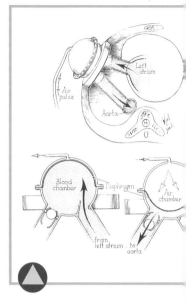

In 1953, DeBakey actually removed the blockage from an artery. This operation had never been done before.

But DeBakey's greatest work was yet to come. In 1960 he began to develop the first artificial heart. In 1966 he successfully **implanted** it in a living body.

DeBakey drew diagrams to show how his artificial heart worked.

Then, in 1988, when he was eighty years old, DeBakey invented a machine called the VAD. It helps a weakened heart pump blood though the body.

Michael DeBakey has performed heart surgery on more than 60,000 people.

Over the years, Michael DeBakey has developed many devices that have saved millions of lives.

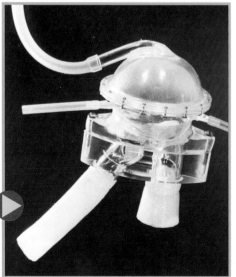

This is the artificial heart DeBakey designed and implanted in 1966.

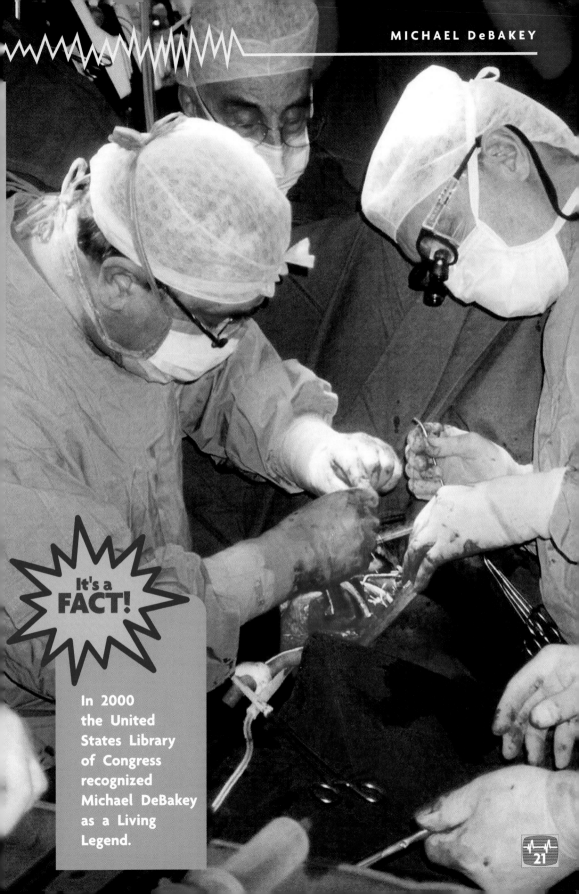

It's a
FACT!

In 2000
the United
States Library
of Congress
recognized
Michael DeBakey
as a Living
Legend.

# CHAPTER 5

# Milestones in Modern Medicine

1820 – Florence Nightingale born in Florence, Italy

1853 – Nightingale travels to Germany to study nursing

1854 – Nightingale and 38 other nurses start work in war hospitals during the Crimean War

1860 – Nightingale starts the Nightingale School for Nurses in London, England

1908 – Michael DeBakey born in Lake Charles, Louisiana

1914 – Jonas Salk born in New York City

1939 – Salk graduates from medical school

1942 – Salk starts influenza vaccine research at the University of Michigan

1942 – DeBakey serves in World War II, establishing first MASH units

1950 – DeBakey develops an artificial artery

1955 – Salk invents a successful polio vaccine

1966 – DeBakey implants an artificial heart into a living body

1988 – DeBakey invents the VAD

# Glossary

| | |
|---|---|
| artificial | not natural |
| branch | a portion or division of a business or profession |
| epidemics | outbreaks of a disease |
| immune | capable of resisting a disease |
| implanted | inserted into a living thing |
| iron lung | a machine that helps people breathe |
| medical profession | the work of healing people |
| organ | a plant or animal structure, such as the heart, that performs some bodily function |
| polio | a very serious virus disease that attacks the nerve cells of the spinal cord |
| surgeon | a doctor who operates on the human body |
| surgery | repairing injuries or correcting diseases by operating on the human body |
| vaccine | material made of a dead or weakened virus that helps the body resist a disease |
| virus | infectious particles that can grow and multiply in the human body and cause disease |

# Index